T0146834

Six Sexy, Simple Steps
for
Dating at 60

Six Sexy, Simple Steps
for
Dating at 60

A Thought-Provoking, Motivational
Narrative for Sexagenarians

Chele Iam

Six Sexy, Simple Steps for Dating at 60
A Thought-Provoking, Motivational Narrative for Sexagenarians

iUniverse books may be ordered through booksellers or by contacting:

iUniverse
1663 Liberty Drive
Bloomington, IN 47403
www.iuniverse.com
1-800-Authors (1-800-288-4677)

Because of the dynamic nature of the Internet, any web addresses or links contained in this book may have changed since publication and may no longer be valid. The views expressed in this work are solely those of the author and do not necessarily reflect the views of the publisher, and the publisher hereby disclaims any responsibility for them.

Any people depicted in stock imagery provided by Thinkstock are models, and such images are being used for illustrative purposes only. Certain stock imagery © Thinkstock.

ISBN: 978-1-5320-0122-2 (sc)
ISBN: 978-1-5320-0121-5 (e)

Library of Congress Control Number: 2016912384

Print information available on the last page.

iUniverse rev. date: 10/21/2016

Six Sexy, Simple Steps for Dating at Sixty invites all Sexagenarians to:

- Be open to new adventures
- Be receptive to fun and exhilaration
- Be joyful and accept the love that is coming your way

"Life is a Dance; be the Dancer!"

The informative stories and steps to dating success are dedicated to you, the Sexy, Spirited Sexagenarians (Sixty+).

Gratitude

Before proceeding on with exciting, useful information for daters in their sixties, I am taking this opportunity to extend gratitude to the incredible young people in my life.

My dedication is to my son Shane and my daughter Tiffany. Without their on-going love and support, I would not have had the tenacity and fortitude to create and write this book.

When I think of all the craziness I have experienced in my sixty plus years of life, I always fall back onto the love and gratefulness I have for my family!

I have married more than once and dated in excess of one hundred and fifty men since turning sixty. It has been my personal experience, as a senior dating in her sixties, that created the premise for **Six Sexy, Simple Steps for Dating at Sixty.**

Of all my accomplishments, my children are my greatest. They have always shown love without judgment. Without a doubt, there were times that judgment should have prevailed.

Shane and Tiffany, thank you both for always letting me be just me – right, wrong or indifferent. I love you both from the bottom of my heart!

Contents

Preface

Six Sexy, Simple Steps for Dating at Sixty is
intended to be a quick, easy read. It is dedicated
to all the loving, single seniors who are ready to
reinvent themselves in the dating world.

We are the Sexagenarians. We are a great
generation with knowledge and understanding.

We continue to make a difference in this
world and we are courageous in living our lives
with richness and joy.

Spiritual treatments and excerpts from
individuals I have come to respect are presented
throughout the book.

If you are frightened to get out there again
and date at age sixty or beyond, dispel your fear

of fright right now. Remember the cliché: "The only thing to fear is fear itself."

Know that you are safe even when you may be vulnerable. Embrace new experiences both positive and negative. These are life's lessons.

It's time to begin living life to its fullest! It's time to break old habits. It's time to create the wonderful dating experiences you desire and deserve.

Please feel free to visit my website: www. stepstodatingat60.love. Let's blog and continue our conversation. It's an on-going process.

The book and blog will give you the tools and confidence you desire to begin your adventure. Enjoy. I wish you only the best!

Introduction

Before jumping into the main content, I want to introduce myself. I am not one who chooses to sit and brag about my awards and accomplishments, however, I realize that it is important for an author to demonstrate credibility.

I thought that dating over one hundred and fifty men in one year at the age of sixty would suffice (a little levity here).

I am a divorced woman who has been fortunate in my life's professional experiences. I am a retired television executive and have worked for both public and network television. I have received numerous awards in journalism, directing, producing, on-air programming, community outreach, mentoring and public speaking.

In addition, I have owned my own self-improvement company mentoring thousands of women around the country.

I want you to know that I am not a psychologist. I am also not a dating expert. One might say I am not the stereotypical dating author because of my age. I am also not Steve Harvey, the self-proclaimed Chief Love Officer, who exudes love and inspiration.

I am, however, a woman who has and continues to date extensively since turning sixty. My experiences are vast and I have learned many valuable lessons and tips to pass on to those of you who are interested in joining the world of dating at sixty. My dating education has been through life's every day experiences.

I have to admit that my writing has a dual purpose. It is not only educational and informational for daters in their sixties, it is also cathartic for me.

I created and now accept the negativity that has come into my life. As I stated earlier, I have been married more than once. I will be elaborating on my last marriage because it was very colorful.

I was fully aware of the many deceitful happenings that my last husband, Good Time Charlie Brown, (not his actual name) brought into our relationship. I wanted my marriage to this man to be everlasting, but this was never going to happen. I was naïve and vulnerable. I truly cared too much.

My first husband and I were together twenty-eight years. He was my childhood sweetheart. I met him at age fifteen and married him at age nineteen.

I feel that this marriage was a success in its own right. It just was not meant to be forever. I do not choose to elaborate on the negatives of this marriage because it was great for many reasons. The two most positive were my children.

Now to continue with the details of my failed marriage to Good Time Charlie Brown. Let's start with him lying to me about being divorced when we met. He maintained this lie for almost two years.

For God's sake, I allowed him to live in my home all this time before finding out that he was not divorced. He was legally separated. In the eyes of the law, this means he was still married. Believe me, he chose to live this lie.

I removed him from my home so many times, it was not even funny. The movers suggested I purchase stock in the moving company. Crazy as it was, I allowed him to return time after time. Insane, you say. Even sane people do insane things. I can attest to that.

I allowed Good Time Charlie Brown to repeatedly come back into my life knowing he had deceived me. I have no excuse except to say I fell in love with him. I thought my love would change him. Not.

The Power of Positivity says that: "When we crave love and romance, we live in our heads. We need to feel special in and out of bed! No one wants *less* passion in a relationship."

My *"Unhappiness"* list in this marriage was long and detailed. Lying about being divorced was only the beginning that lead to the end for me.

After Good Time Charlie Brown eventually divorced his second wife, they still continued to communicate and even see one another when the circumstance presented itself. She called him with regularity; he called her with regularity.

At this point, we were engaged and then married while all of this transpired. He actually admitted to me that he used a fake name for her in his cell phone. I don't know why. I never checked his phone messages. It must be a trait of cheaters. Do you think?

His ex-wife is also a piece of work. Good Time Charlie Brown and his ex-wife deserve each other. She actually called my phone and cussed me out because she said I was living with "her" husband. She went as far as sending me copies of every card and love letter Good Time Charlie Brown ever gave her. She mailed them to me so I would receive them on the day we married. Nice, huh?

What kind of a person does such a malicious thing?

He actually called me by his ex-wife's name several times on our honeymoon. I see you rolling your eyes. Not a great way to start a new marriage! Good Time Charlie Brown told me it was "No big deal; I was making too much of him calling me her name." Are you kidding me? What kind of fool was I?

I still ask myself this question. I have to say that I was "*insanely*" in love with a man who caused me more grief than any one person deserves.

You might ask why he married me if he still appeared to be in love with his second wife. I continually asked him the same question. He never gave me a straight answer. He merely proclaimed his love for me. Just a big "duh" on my behalf. I wanted to believe that love is always forgiving. I felt I had to make my *Golden Years Marriage* work, but enough is enough. Right?

I was co-dependent. No more to say. I was already invested in that word called marriage. What was so ridiculous about this is the fact that there was never anything for me to be co-dependent about in this marital relationship.

I had my own home to return to and I paid for all of my own expenses. I paid for my haircuts, my nails, the gym and the list goes on. What was there to be co-dependent about?

He did pay for our travels because he wanted a travel partner. He never showed every day acts of kindness, such as putting gas in my car or taking care of the maintenance. A man knows how to treat a woman well by doing kind, manly, things for her with regularity. I was a lone soldier the majority of the time.

I want all of you reading this to realize that you are more likely in better shape than you think you are when it comes to removing yourself from an unhealthy situation. It must be done! There is no other choice.

This marriage caused me grief, depression and ill health. The want and will to thrive and survive diminishes when depression rules your life. This is what happened to me.

Be conscious of the negative signs. Let your intuition guide you. This stands true both in marriage and dating. Of course, abuse is never acceptable. Verbal abuse is just as wrong as physical abuse.

I let my love for this man rule my thoughts of permanently leaving him. How do we love individuals who do not know how to love us fully and unconditionally? We have to make healthy choices and move out of negativity when this is the case. If we do not, the end result will not be a healthy or positive one.

I tell you my story so that you will immediately identify the signs I *chose* to ignore. If you are having doubts about a person you are falling in love with, you might want to do a background check on him or her. It would have made my life easier.

Today, when I see negative signs, I do not ignore them. There are lots of lessons to be learned here. I do believe everyone comes into our lives for a reason. Think about it. We do learn something from every date, acquaintance, mate we have ever met. You may not always like what you learn, but the lesson is there.

Life can be simplified, especially when we are starting a new beginning and dating as a Sexagenarian.

My purpose is to present actual stories that have been problematic, some unreal and some very humorous for me in life and in the dating world. I share them with you so you will know ahead of time how to handle or avoid some crazy, uncomfortable situations.

If I can make your life easier and more fulfilling as you begin your sexy sixty journey into dating again, then I have accomplished what I have set out to do in writing ***Six Sexy, Simple Steps for Dating at Sixty.***

Quick Read

It's a fun, easy read. I have quoted and referenced individuals throughout who have influenced me.

There are many wonderful authors in the self-help, motivational reading arena, but I do not know of any at sixty years of age who have dated over one hundred and fifty men in one year. This is why I chose to write for a specific audience, the "Sexagenarians."

The ***Six Sexy, Simple Steps for Dating at Sixty*** will be interjected throughout all of my true life stories. Some stories may seem a bit unusual, even unbelievable, but I promise you, I lived through each and every one of them. My advice will give insight into the positive approach for making your experiences great ones.

Why Write Six Sexy, Simple Steps for Dating at Sixty?

First of all, why not? No one has ever conveyed this type of information to Sexagenarians. No one thinks about how the baby boomer population gets itself back into the dating world after divorce or being widowed.

We are a vibrant population and we just need to receive some simple steps to guide us and increase our confidence as we enter into the world of dating. There are many of us out there in this age range. With my advice and simple steps, I am certain you will be successfully dating in no time.

I am here to motivate you. I am here to educate the new dating population of men and women who are in their sixties.

Six Sexy, Simple Steps for Dating at Sixty is short and to the point for a reason. It's not a novel. It gives you advice to use now.

Master the steps; enjoy the stories. Get acquainted with what you may encounter. Have faith; believe in yourself and begin dating. Live in the moment with excitement and curiosity. The possibility of love might even enter the picture. Nothing wrong with that.

You will receive insight to successfully and enjoyably date at this great age and stage of life, but you have to be open to my suggestions. If you are asking why dating in your sixties is any different than any other age, then you will definitely need to continue reading.

Get the thought out of your mind that you are too old to date. You are as old as you feel. Do not let the number of your age define you.

Those who say: "I am old" will be old. You have a choice to live with happiness and vitality or be a grumpy, old person. The time is now to live your life. Just keep in mind that *sixty is sexy!*

Today, I realize I allowed the blatant fear of being alone to rule my choices. I have always been described as a strong, confident woman. Even strong, confident women make mistakes when it comes to love.

It was after excessively dating that I put a message out to the universe to bring a special man into my life. I was sent Good Time Charlie Brown. Oh yeah, he was special alright. We need to be very careful what we ask for because I got exactly what I asked for and it wasn't all good. It was a lot of "Not So Good!"

I have always been attracted to the narcissistic, egocentric types. This is Good Time Charlie Brown. I know what you are thinking and you are right. Five and one-half years later, we divorced. No longer do I desire this type of man in my life!

Know that passion can be killed by dishonesty. Do not ever forget this. My mantra is "Love me for all I am; Love me for all I am not." Be open. Be real. Be candid. Do not let romance sweep you off your feet. I am confident my suggestions will benefit you. I invite you to visit my website: www.stepstodatingat60.love. Let's talk; let's blog. Let's learn from each other!

The **Six Sexy, Simple Steps for Dating at Sixty** will be interjected throughout my true life stories. Some stories may seem a bit unbelievable, but, without a doubt, I lived through each and every one of them. I feel certain my simple steps will give you the insight you desire to enhance your dating experiences.

True life can actually be more exciting than fiction. I am a woman in my sixties who has made it to this magical time in life. I have not reached my destination. I am on this wondrous journey with you!

Life is awesome. Why shouldn't it be? I can tell you that I am a living, breathing, happy person experiencing the fun and excitement that I have created. It is by no means the end of the road for me. This time of life is enlightening and adventuresome. It's what I choose to make it. You can do the same!

Quoting Victor Hugo: "Be like the bird, who halting in his flight on limb too slight, feels it give way beneath him. Yet sings, knowing he hath wings."

Why shouldn't I feel great? I am free like a bird. I have my wings to fly and I am free to make good choices. You can do the same.

I still have lots of hair to color; I have all of my teeth (and they are white and straight) and I am healthy and physically fit.

My dates were few in my youth, but I certainly made up for it in my sixties. It's time to venture out into the world of dating and explore new avenues. I am ready to share my encounters and knowledge with you, so you can have a great time creating your path to positive dating.

Our population, the sixties, seventies and older are living longer more wondrous lives. The folks who I have spoken to over the years tell me a major void exists in their lives. They desire love and companionship. Sitting on the couch watching television will not manifest a mate for you.

I will not let the baby boomers be considered the forgotten generation. We were trailblazers in our day. What's stopping us from blazing new trails in our *sexy sixties?*

The dating books, videos and movies are generally directed to the young. We are in our sixties; we are, without a doubt, the young at heart!

See Your Greatness

Ladies and gentlemen, **Six Sexy, Simple Steps for Dating at Sixty** is directed to all of you in your sixties, seventies and beyond.

Men and women alike are not kind to themselves as they age. We are a society that often gives more merit to the external appearance of an individual than to the heart and soul. I cannot change the world, but I can ask one person, you, to look in a mirror and see your greatness.

The time is now to be grateful. Life is pretty spectacular; you are *sexy* and *sixty*! Just look at all the technological advances you have experienced in the past sixty years.

If you have lost all of your teeth, you do not need to panic. There are dentists who can beautify your mouth with false teeth or implants in just hours. Your teeth can look better than they did in your twenties.

The same stands true for loss of hair. As we age, many men and women lose their hair. It's just a fact of life. This does not have to be a problem either. Your choices are many.

You can choose to rejuvenate your hair with one of numerous products on the market. Another choice is to live with the stylishly bald look that is fashionable today for both men and women. You can purchase a wig. No excuse to not like yourself because your hair is not the same as it was when you were a younger person. It can be even better because so many choices are availed to you.

It's a Road

It may not be the yellow brick road, but it will be your road to travel. You might even find true love. Be open to what is in store for you.

It takes time. Do not ever settle because you are sixty. For that matter, never settle at any age. Been there; done that. Why do I think you may have also been there and done that?

Don't fly through life going ninety in a forty-mile speed zone. The results won't be positive. You are in your sixties. You know what type of person you want in your life. You also know what type of person you *don't* want in your life. Slow down. Be selective. Now is the time to use your wisdom.

Too many of us choose the road of life that brings us pain and sorrow. Whether it is intentional or not doesn't matter. Once we have made the choice, we need to decide if we want to stay or move on to a happier, more fulfilling road.

We can always change our direction. Remember, it's a choice.

Our hearts often tell us to proceed through the red traffic light even though we know better. Guilty as charged. I always made excuses for my mistakes.

Does this ring a bell for any of you? I now know that my mistakes were and continue to be lessons in life. We have to learn from our lessons or discontent and unhappiness will continue as we date the wrong people.

We often feel it's better to stick with what we know rather than to end a bad relationship and start again. Is it because we just do not want to travel the road alone again? Perhaps. This was something I had to deal with and eventually overcome.

Patience is a Virtue

When looking for true love, many of us are not too patient. It can, and more than likely, will be a time-consuming process. Know that it can also be an interesting and enjoyable process.

You are sixty. You are living with the gift of life. No one knows the number of days you will have on earth. Live with quality and conviction. Live life in the now!

Be grateful for every person who comes into your life. There is a reason. Just one person can lead you to another and then another, and with patience, you can find true love.

Rarely does love ignite and manifest after just one date. Lust and attraction may spark your interest, but come on, this is only for a minute.

Are you looking for long-term love or short-term lust? It's your decision. I vote for long-term love.

A Bit of Personal History

I share my personal history and background throughout so you will have a better understanding of who I am and the road I have travelled to bring me to this juncture today. If someone would have told me fifteen years ago that I would be sitting at my computer writing a book today that gives dating advice to people sixty years of age and older, I would have said the obvious. Are you nuts? So it is and here I am.

Dating is a process; it takes time. Truth be told, it can be considered a numbers game or a game of chance.

Life is a journey. Dating in your sixties can be one of the most enlightening parts of this wondrous journey.

You now have maturity; you now have wisdom. Why would you choose to rush into any situation that may appear negative? You know the type of person you desire in your life. Don't ever settle for anyone less.

The late, great Robin Williams said: "I used to think that the worst thing in life was to end up alone. The worst thing in life is to end up with people who make you feel alone." I could not agree more.

I felt more alone in my last marriage than I do today living alone with my two awesome Chihuahuas. I live a happy, fulfilled life. It is wonderful to live without judgment and chaos.

I love meeting new people and I continue dating, but I am not rushing into a love relationship with any one person at this time. I will know when the time is right and I am willing to wait for that special man. I know he is out there waiting for me as well. I encourage you to do the same.

Change is Healthy

I have certainly had my share of life's changes. I moved from my home town of Huntington Beach, California to Salt Lake City, Utah with my family.

The move was an advancement in my children's dad's career. As a dutiful wife of twenty plus years, I packed up our family and left all that I ever knew. I left life-long friends and family. It was not easy to make this move.

I soon came to find out that change is healthy. I began meeting new friends and fell in love with the four seasons of beautiful Utah.

After settling the children in to their new environment and putting our home together, I sought employment and was offered a great position in the world of public television in Salt Lake City.

After three and one-half years, I was offered a position at ABC in Salt Lake City to head a newly formed department. I became their Director of Public Affairs and Special Projects. It was fantastic.

It took me ten years to obtain my Bachelor of Arts degree from Cal-State University at Long Beach. Television broadcasting was my quest.

After high school, I went to work Monday through Friday, as a secretary, for the Chief Executive Office in Los Angeles. I went to Cal State University in Long Beach every night after work. My tenacity and perseverance made me who I am today. It was all worth it.

We are always changing. Life is always changing. I have been an ambitious person my entire life. I did not grow up with money. I grew up with lots of love and that is what mattered.

When I had to seek employment at fifteen years of age to help my family, I just did it. We do whatever it is that we need to do to make life work for us.

My youth consisted of school and work. That is what I knew and so that is what I did. No questions asked.

We all have a story or two about our past. Our past makes us who we are, but we now need to live in the present. Time does not go backwards.

It's time to fast forward. When I decided to make another change in my life, it was after divorcing my children's dad.

I visited my son who was living in Scottsdale, Arizona. Before I knew it, I was sold on moving to another state where the only person I knew was my son.

I decided it was a lot easier to shovel sun than snow. Time for another change in life.

I was officially a divorcee. I was told by the naysayers that at *my age,* I should not be making such a drastic move. Well, as soon as you tell me not to do something, that is when I do it. Oh yeah.

Why shouldn't I make this change? I am healthy, well-maintained and still full of vim and vigor. I read that Scottsdale was one of the top cities for senior dating. All the more reason to make the change.

I was married the majority of my life, so this change of venue was just another adventure for me. I was actually looking forward to it.

The Internet

Having only a couple of dates in my life, I wasn't certain what to expect about the world of dating as it is today, especially for a senior citizen.

I did know that Internet dating was going to be an avenue I would have to pursue. We lose our network connections when we retire or move to a new state. So, let the journey and excitement of Internet dating begin.

The first thing you need to do before going on an Internet site is to decide which site is best for you. A plethora of sites are available for seniors: Our Time.com, Senior People Meet.com, and Plenty of Fish.com are just a few that work well.

Before moving to Arizona, my daughter put me on a selected Internet dating site. She took a few photos of me to post and then we built my profile.

A day before moving to Arizona, we checked the Internet site to see if I had any messages. It was unbelievable, to say the least. I had twenty-six messages waiting for me. I began communicating with a few different men and when I arrived in Scottsdale, my dating escapades began.

Men were coming out of the woodwork. Shame on those who told me that dating at my age would be difficult. They had no idea what they were talking about.

Let the fun begin. They were old; they were young; they were short; they were tall; they had long hair; they were bald; they were chunky; they were skinny; they were comedy writers; they were entrepreneurs; they were millionaire eccentrics; they were doctors; they were lawyers; they were battalion fire chiefs; they were muscle men trainers and, of course, some were just plain old cheapskate idiots. It was totally unreal!

Okay, are you ready for this? In one year of Internet dating, I dated one hundred and fifty-eight men. It was amazing and amusing and *true.* Thus, the reason for writing **Six Sexy, Simple Steps for Dating at Sixty.**

You cannot pay for this type of education. I deserve the title: "*Senior Serial Dater.*" Do you know of any person at sixty years of age who has had this type of experience? If you do, please have that person blog me. I do not think there are too many of us. It would be fun sharing stories.

So, once again naysayers, "Shame, Shame." It's obvious they did not know what they were talking about when they doubted my dating success at age sixty.

I want to say I loved *almost* every minute of it. It became my full-time job my first year in Arizona.

Honesty, Honesty, Honesty

Well, as interesting as Internet dating was, and still is at times, I ended up meeting Good Time Charlie Brown at a dance club for mature singles. The dance club was called Calculated Couples.

This group no longer exists, but it was an awesome, safe place to dance and meet new people.

Some folks prefer meeting at a bar. I have never been the type of woman who goes to a bar alone. Now for many, the bar scene works. I am not here to condone or condemn. Do what is right for you.

When I was told about Calculated Couples in Scottsdale, I was excited. After all, life is a dance. I was ready to be the dancer.

As I mentioned, this is where I met Good Time Charlie Brown. I need you to know that I am a petite woman who is naturally well endowed. This particular evening, I dressed much more alluring than usual. This is what actually attracted Good Time Charlie Brown to me.

I was my own worst enemy because my dress showed too much cleavage. You see, we create our own situations. Please keep this in mind.

It's time that I tell you some great things about Good Time Charlie Brown. It couldn't have all been bad or I would not have been attracted to him. It would not be fair to only highlight his negatives.

He is a very nice looking man with swagger. In addition, he has style, is a great dresser and dancer and enjoys travel as much as I do. Adding to the list is his great sense of humor and outgoing personality. We did have that thing called chemistry. No denying that.

Even though chemistry is a major element in a relationship, it alone will not keep a relationship or marriage together. You have to connect on many different levels.

The positive qualities of Good Time Charlie Brown bonded me to him. We did have fun, laughter and many great times together. Unfortunately, I did not consider the importance of honesty and integrity until it was too late.

What do I look for in a potential mate today? Of course, honesty and integrity are essential traits. Open, healthy communication is also a necessity. Everything else follows.

My list does not end there. A man who is selfless, loving, caring, romantic, successful, trustworthy, reliable, fun and knows the definition of unconditional love is a keeper in my book. I, like most women, also appreciate chivalry.

True love is always forgiving. True love is to be shared and nurtured in both good times and bad.

It is said that there are three types of people who come into our lives: Those who have helped you in difficult times; those who have left you in difficult times; and those who put you in difficult times. Good Time Charlie Brown both left and put me in some of my most difficult times. Did he know better? I believe he did. Was he remorseful? I don't know.

Be clear about what you desire in your mate. I was not. I am not the type of woman who usually dresses provocatively, but this is how I dressed the night I met Good Time Charlie Brown. I got what I asked for. Am I clear here?

I saw what I wanted to see in this man. I did not see him for who he actually is – an egocentric, selfish, narcissistic man. He marched to the beat of his own drum doing what he wanted to do when he wanted to do it. As long as I followed, all was well.

Buyer Beware. I tell you my story so you will learn from my mistakes. Do you really think I was unaware of his negative qualities before marrying him? I was very aware. I kicked him out of my home numerous times. The movers told me I should buy stock in their moving company.

As I previously mentioned, you are now on a new road of life. When you see a red flag, stop! Do not go through the barricade. You will suffer the consequences. I certainly did.

Break the Cycle

In 1992, author John Gray wrote the popular book, Men are from Mars Women are from Venus. It's a practical guide for improving commitment and getting to know what you want in a relationship.

John Gray says: "When a man listens to a woman's feelings without getting angry and frustrated, he gives her a wonderful gift."

"He makes it safe for her to express herself. She feels heard and understood. She is then able to give a man the loving trust, acceptance, appreciation, admiration, approval and encouragement he needs." This is so true!

Even though Men are from Mars Women are from Venus is an older book, I believe it is still useful and fun to read today. I suggest that if you can find a copy in a used book store, buy it. You will enjoy it for years to come.

So, we all know the male and female species are very different. The more we learn about one another, the better our relationships will be. In spite of all of our differences, we find we can't always live with each other, but we don't want to live without one another either.

So, let's choose to learn more about one another so our relationships will be fabulous.

I went through a great deal of spiritual training and guidance when I chose to divorce Good Time Charlie Brown. I told my guides that I always followed my heart in my relationships.

One of my spiritual guides explained that this was only one body part to follow. My guide's name was Maya. She is a beautiful woman from India. She was so insightful. She told me I needed to start using my head and break the cycle of the type of men I was attracted to, dated and married in my past. This was one big "Wow!" Of course, I knew she was right.

She also told me to use my intuition. I am very intuitive, but I have often chosen to ignore my intuition, which has caused me much of my grief.

If something does not feel right, it more than likely is not. A good person should be a R.A.T. Do not take this acronym in the literal sense. It stands for *"Respectful, Accountable and Trustworthy."*

These are mandatory traits when you are looking for a great, everlasting partner. If you are looking for a fun, one-time date, then maybe these traits will not be as significant. You decide.

As I previously mentioned, I fancied the narcissistic men. I now choose to break this cycle. This type of man no longer fits into my life. It would be ridiculous to continue dating this type of person.

Think about the type of partners you have brought into your life. Did they bring you negativity? If so, you too, must break the cycle now.

Good Time Charlie Brown admitted to me that he has always been a selfish person; he comes first. He does what he wants to do when he wants to do it. I guess, like so many other women, I thought I could change him. Not.

The sad part is I will always care about him. Some of the worst things he did to me, I will not discuss. This is something I will have to figure out as I continue on my own road of life.

I knew then and I know now, it's time for change. It's time to break the cycle.

Be aware of a person's negative characteristics. Do not think you can change a person. At our age, it is a difficult thing to do. This is why it is important for you to look for an individual who has the positive traits you see and know to be genuine.

Write a list of all the traits you desire in a mate. Look at it daily; add to it daily. You attract what you put out there. It's true!

STEP 1

MEN ARE HUNTERS; LET THEM HUNT

Some may agree; some may disagree with this statement. I believe it to be true.

Men are visual creatures. This is how the hunt begins. I have been told by many men that women in our age group can be very aggressive. If women know what they want, they go after it.

Some men like aggressive women, but for the most part, men like to be the pursuers when beginning a relationship. Of course, chemistry is always an essential element.

If you are a strong, independent person, be that person. There should never be trickery when dating. It needs to be real. It needs to be honest. It needs to be sincere.

Get to know one another. If you are both feeling an attraction, engage in a good exchange of questions and answers. Look into each other's eyes and show interest in the conversation.

Do not discuss every experience of life you have ever had. Remember, it's your first date. It takes time and trust as you get to know one another.

A conversation needs to be between two people. It is very uncomfortable for one person to not only ask all the questions, but then answer them as well. It's important to keep communication flowing. You cannot do this if you are a silent dater. The same stands true if you are a verbose dater. The art of conversation is like playing volleyball. Toss it back and forth.

If the date went well, let the man call you to discuss a second date. It really works better this way. Women today often take the lead. This can be detrimental in the long run.

If the conversation is boring and not going the way you would like it to or if the chemistry is lacking, keep a smile on your face. A little courtesy goes a long way.

If there is interest between the two of you, and you are thinking about a more serious relationship than just dating, discuss your past history as it relates to children or parents who may be living with you.

Are your current circumstances going to blend with your intended partner? Will there be an eventual problem? It could be the beginning to the end if it is not discussed in the early stages of dating while you are getting to know one another.

Think Before You Speak

You have talked, texted, e-mailed and are now ready to meet live and in person. This is assuming you have met the person on the Internet. This can be the most exciting time in this venture. For some, it has proven to be the worst time.

For a moment, let's go back to "Honesty, Honesty, Honesty." If either men or women lie *severely* about their age or weight, they can cause themselves major problems. A year or two or a pound or two should not be the end of the world. We have all done this one time or another.

I have been told by too many men that they walked out on their dates when the women came into their meeting place weighing fifty plus pounds heavier than in their photographs. How humiliating! Do *not* put yourself in this situation.

The same has happened when men and women alike lie *severely* about their age. Do you really think your date is not going to notice that you are twenty years older than in your photograph? These are major "No, No's."

Remember, men are hunters. Initially, they are attracted to a woman's picture. The profile on an internet site is secondary. I have tested this theory over and over again. It's true.

Women also look at a photograph, but the profile has equal relevance for "most" women.

Men, just as women, have an expectation. They see your picture and anticipate it to look the way it is posted. This is only right. It must be a recent or relatively recent photograph. Don't start out being a deceitful dater. The one who will be hurt the most from this unfortunate first meeting will be you.

It is time to move forward and discuss the positive remarks versus the negative remarks on your first date. Simply stated: "Think Before You Speak."

To both men and women, if you cannot say something complimentary on the first date, then just be respectful. Try: "It's nice to meet you" and then keep the date short. With courtesy, excuse yourself. Never just walk out.

How hard is it to be polite to another human being for fifteen minutes of your life? I promise you, kindness is always reciprocated.

Be true to who you are and present yourself without lies and deceit. Do not knowingly misrepresent yourself and expect the end result to be a positive one.

Some individuals feel that off-color, sexual jokes will break the ice on a first date. It usually will break the date rather than break the ice. It's not appropriate.

I have dated some men who thought they were being cute by making stupid comments about my nail polish color, hair or the number of bracelets I was wearing. Are you kidding me? I said their comments were "stupid" not cute nor complimentary.

How many dates did I go on with each of them after the initial date? None.

You are just getting to know a person. You need to be on your best behavior. Keep the conversation positive and flowing. It makes for a better date for both of you. If you are inconsiderate or impolite, the first date will definitely lead to the last.

In Arizona, there are numerous groups for mature, single adults to go to and meet one another. They are actually referred to as "Meetup" groups. Meetups cover the gamut of interests for our age group. They include: wine tasting, art exhibits, spiritual get-togethers, book clubs, hiking, dancing and the list goes on. Just click Meetup in your area on the Internet and see if these groups are available.

I belong to a great Meetup called Valley Singles 50+, Don't Do It Alone. The President and founder of this group is an incredible woman. Her name is Debbie D. and her meetup group is her passion.

She has been coordinating get-togethers for mature Valley singles for years. She creates a safe, inviting environment for all who attend her events.

Let me just say that not all Meetup groups are the same. I attended another one in Scottsdale that was very uninviting and self-serving. Check the various ones out to see which group and leadership best meet your needs.

I have a "Think before You Speak" date from a gentleman I met at one of Debbie's Meetup events. Here comes the story about "too many bracelets."

Let's call him Aaron. He invited me to Happy Hour at a Scottsdale restaurant. Conversation was just beginning when he began counting the number of bangle bracelets on my right arm.

He actually had the audacity to chastise me for wearing "too many," in his opinion. Our Happy Hour conversation was not happy for me. He just focused on my excessive bangles. I am not kidding. What a great way to meet, greet and impress someone. Wrong!

I told him that the number of bangles I chose to wear was none of his business. The date ended shortly thereafter this conversation. Aaron was never to be seen again.

Out of necessity, I have become a stronger woman today. I never intentionally try to hurt anyone with my words. If I am hurt, however, that protective guard comes up. Please note: my date may not have appreciated what I told him, but he was rude and his comments were inconsiderate and unnecessary.

I did take a moment and remembered my mantra: "Think Before I Speak." Then I expressed my unhappy feelings to this man. This was not a great way to impress a woman.

STEP 2

IT'S ALL ABOUT CHEMISTRY

The Law of Attraction is another way to describe chemistry. Simply stated, it's when two people are attracted to one another. It's either there or it's not.

Something just happens when you meet that "right" person. You get all giddy, lightheaded and happy. These are such wonderful, amazing feelings. You never want them to end.

There is something very sexy and exciting to say about chemistry.

I had major chemistry with Goodtime Charlie Brown. In spite of all the negatives he brought into my life, I cannot ever deny my attraction to him. Go figure.

We try and ignore the negatives in our relationships when we have strong chemistry. It took a lot for me to be real about my life and future with him because the Law of Attraction prevailed throughout the good, the bad and the ugly times we had together.

Since my divorce to Good Time Charlie Brown, I have had a couple of other strong attractions in the dating world, but I proceeded in and then out of them with caution. They were not meant to be.

I, personally, do need chemistry before going beyond one or two dates with a gentleman. I also listen to the words spoken to me while I look for signs of narcissism. It can be a make or break situation at this point in time.

Think about what is important to you. What traits do you want in your man or woman? It's important to write them down and look at them each day. I stress the realization of this process. Just do it! Add to the list regularly.

I believe we all desire good chemistry, but there is more! Keep the list of affirmations at hand and as a positive reminder. Look at it often. Speak the affirmations out loud.

I remind myself to do this daily and I continually repeat: "I desire a man to be: *Selfless, Honest, Have Integrity, Be Respectful, Be Kind, Be Caring, Be Genuine, Show Unconditional Love, Be Romantic, Have His Own Success, Have A Great Sense of Humor and Be an Overall Good Guy!*" I don't think these qualities are too much to ask for in a great mate.

Love authorities tell us that we should be able to come up with at least one hundred and one positive traits when describing our perfect soul mate. This is my beginning. Stop reading for a moment and start writing your list now.

STEP 3

BE YOUR BEST ON THE FIRST DATE SO IT WON'T BE YOUR LAST

You may have only one opportunity to impress that special person. The old saying: "The world is a stage and we are all actors and actresses" stands true especially when meeting someone new for the first time.

We always need to be ourselves in the best way possible. This means be showered and groomed before going on your date. If you are coming from the gym or work and your clothes are soiled and smell, go home and shower. Put on clean, appropriate clothes for the occasion. If time does not permit, call your intended date and ask if it is okay to be late. If it does not work, then ask to reschedule.

I have had some experiences that were unbelievably inappropriate, so this is why I share this information with you.

I feel that all first-time dates should take place in public venues. This is for safety purposes.

I had a date set to meet a new gentleman at a local restaurant near my home.

He walked in to the restaurant lobby to meet me and I almost turned around and left on the spot. He was in gym shorts and a sweaty tank top with disgusting sweat stains under his arms. He tried giving me a hug as we greeted, but I wasn't having it. Are you kidding me? I had a glass of water and told him I was unable to stay. He looked shocked, but said "Okay." He truly did not get it. Whew, I could not leave quickly enough.

Time for an accolade for Good Time Charlie Brown. He always dressed well and appropriate for any occasion. I have to give credit where credit is due to this man. That was a quality of his that attracted me to him.

I have had dates with many men who have flown in from out of state. Of course, they stayed in local hotels.

One of my more fun-filled events was meeting a gentleman cowboy who flew in from Aspen, Colorado to meet me. He came in for the week.

He actually knew more about Arizona than I did at this point in time. He told me to follow his lead. It was like nothing I had ever done before.!

We went to wonderful restaurants in the Valley and in Scottsdale. He even gave me horseback lessons at a dude ranch. We had a crazy, whirlwind week. It was unreal because we did it the Aspen cowboy way. Keep reading because it only gets better.

He designated a happy nickname for himself and it was even on his license plate. I wish I could share it with you, but to protect his identity, I will have to refrain.

This gentleman topped my list of eccentric dates. He was very accomplished in his own right and I found him to be more than fascinating. I was captivated by his eccentricities.

He selected all the restaurants we would go to before coming to Arizona. He also selected all the appetizers, salads, entrees and desserts for every meal at these restaurants. I had no say in the matter.

He would order four or five appetizers; two or three salads; three or four entrees and several desserts. This was just for the two of us.

His reason for ordering this gargantuan amount of food was that he felt food should be sampled in small portions. He would say, "Just take a bite from each dish." Wow!

All that I could think about, as we carried numerous leftover bags back to my home after each dinner, is "I wonder how many starving children could have benefitted from the amount of money spent on this dining experience." It was unbelievable!

I love the mantra: "Waste not, want not," but after a while, I could not look at another leftover.

Well, you might think that this would top my list of dating highlights, but it does not. I have an even better one that I shared with cowboy.

Are you ready? This cowboy knew how to dress well and did for the majority of restaurants we visited. The end of the week was coming near for cowboy's visit. So hang on tight; change was on its way.

He made reservations for us at one of the most upscale restaurants in Scottsdale, the Ocean Club. I told him I was not interested in dining out again. I had enough leftovers to feed an army. In addition, his eccentric ways were exhausting me.

If my over-the-top dining experiences weren't enough, he wanted to take me shopping and change my style of dress. No more. I had enough.

Well, he was not happy with me at this point and I knew it. He asked if I would go out with him this one last time before he went home. I agreed because I knew he would be leaving the next day. Ocean Club, here we come.

This is the best one. I told him I would meet him at the restaurant. It did not seem to bother him. I did this so I could leave early if I felt it appropriate. Believe me, it ended up being more than appropriate to leave early.

Cowboy arrived in old, battered cowboy chaps, dirty old boots, worn blue jeans and an old weathered cowboy hat. I asked him where the horse was corralled. He did not respond.

The hostesses, at the front desk, had shocked looks on their faces when they saw him. This is the Ocean Club, for God's sake!

I was aghast, but I would not let him know it because I would not allow him to make a fool out of me.

I turned and greeted him and then introduced him to the hostesses as one of the original cowboys from the wild, wild west. The girls uncomfortably laughed and escorted us to our table. I was surprised we were not asked to leave because of the restaurant's dress code. I guess money is money.

We ate in silence. Everyone in the restaurant stared at him. It was not my problem. I was now done with cowboy. Did he dress like this intentionally? Without a doubt!

When you are in the dating world, expect some unusual, bizarre and sometimes off-the-wall things to happen. I can use these adjectives for everything that occurred the week I dated cowboy. None of it was harmful. It was just unusual and different, to say the least. What an experience!

Some dates might offend you. Be strong; be polite, if possible, and leave an uncomfortable situation, if it arises. Never take the unusual dates too serious unless your intuition tells you otherwise.

Some of my dating experiences may have been a bit extreme. Lucky me. If you are a sensitive individual and would be easily offended, think twice before going on the Internet to date. The same holds true for being set up by a friend or colleague.

Dating can be fun; it can be exciting. It can also cause discomfort at times. I believe the good times far outweigh the bad times. Just remember to always "Be Your Best On a First Date, So It Won't Be Your Last."

STEP 4

SHOW INTEREST; BE RESPECTFUL

In my opinion, this is one of the most important steps. As a woman, I am going to take responsibility for saying I feel men are usually the guilty ones when it comes to not engaging in "productive" conversation on first dates. This was touched on earlier. Let me elaborate.

Ask questions; show interest in your date. It's respectful. It can also make the person feel more comfortable.

I was recently on a date with a man where there was no chemistry. This is fine. He was a boring, but nice man. I was more than ready to make my exit. We just did not click.

All that he actually knew about me was my first name and that I was from Scottsdale. I could tell you his whole life's story. I told him during this date that we were not a connection. Adios.

Often times, men are merely trying to impress women with their professional lives, their income, cars and whatever else they feel is important to share with a woman on the first date.

A little background about oneself is important for both parties. It's healthy banter. It's how each of you get to know one another. No one should dominate the conversation.

I would have appreciated this gentleman asking me a few questions about my children, my professional life, my interests. This did not happen. We ended our dinner date when he told me the woman in his last relationship was twenty-five years his junior. All that I could say besides "Good Night" was "Wow."

Most women will sit attentively listening to men discuss their lives and accomplishments. They won't interject unless men give them an opening.

If a woman is shy and reserved, she may sit the whole evening with a smile on her face saying nothing about herself. This is not right.

The opposite can be true for women being more talkative than men. It can go either way.

Keep in mind that there are two of you who are trying to meet and greet with as much comfort as possible on the first date. Both of you are looking for that common bond. It can be dynamic. It could also be disastrous if there is a lack of interest or respect for one another.

Regardless of the chemistry, every date can be pleasant if both daters put forth the effort to engage in some light conversation.

Ladies and gentlemen, whether or not you fall in lust or love on the first date, is irrelevant. What is relevant is for both of you to acknowledge one another with respect and a "thank you" at the conclusion of the date.

Now for another of my dating stories. All of my meet and greets are at cafes or restaurants. This is for a reason. First of all, these are public places. Second of all, it does not take that long to have a cup of coffee if you need to make an early departure.

I had two very similar dates on two separate occasions. They were "coffee dates" at the same local restaurant. Many men, and women as well, prefer to meet for just a cup of coffee.

It does not take but a minute to see if there is a connection. There might not be immediate chemistry, but there can be a cerebral connection. What do each of you have to lose? It's fifteen minutes of your life and a cup of coffee.

I began my road in broadcasting as an investigative journalist, so I find interest and intrigue in almost everyone I meet. The coffee date works at times for me. It should be relatively short. This is its intent.

These two times, the coffee dates were not cutting it! My dates were with highly-educated men who were psychologists.

For reference sake, I will refer to Dater Number One as Psychologist A. Dater Number Two will be Psychologist B.

Psychologist A met me in the entrance of Paradise Bakery. He bought me my cup of coffee and we sat down at 10:30 a.m. to begin our meet and greet.

He did not like coffee or tea, so he sat at the table without any type of beverage. Social skills? There were none. When we were done, I needed a stiff drink.

Two and one-half hours later, with a stale cup of coffee, I continued listening to him. The lunch hour had come and gone and he did not have the courtesy to ask if I would like a sandwich or a bowl of soup. For God's sake, we were sitting this whole time in Paradise Bakery. What was he thinking? I know what I was thinking. So long Psychologist A.

Now let me introduce you to Psychologist B. It's true. Both of these men were psychologists. I know all psychologists are not like the two I dated. If you are a psychologist, please do not take offense. These were like two peas in a pod. I should have dated them at the same time so I did not have to waste my time dating them separately.

Psychologist B arrived at Paradise Bakery ahead of me. In case you are wondering if I own stock in Paradise Bakery, I do not. It's just a convenient location for me to have a cup of coffee with a man I have never met before.

Psychologist B was sitting at the table when I arrived. He did stand up to greet me, but he did not offer to buy me a $1.25 cup of coffee.

This was different. Invite a woman to a coffee shop and then expect her to buy her own cup of coffee. Unbelievable! What an impression he made. Not a favorable one!

He called and e-mailed me a few times after this meeting. It was to no avail. It's hard to believe that these two men, in the same profession, were so similar and yet so out of touch with exhibiting social grace. Just coincidental, I imagine.

I will often put the following phrase in my profile write-up on Internet sites: *"I am not a nurse with a purse."* Most men get it; some do not. I thank my friend, Penny, for sharing this mantra with me. It describes who I am today.

When a man is too cheap and inconsiderate to buy a woman a cup of coffee when he asks her out on the date, I say: "So long!" Psychologist B needed to see a psychologist.

Come on guys, if a woman is polite enough to listen to your self-absorbed conversation for over two hours, the least you can do is buy her a cup of coffee. A bagel would be a huge bonus.

Another issue of great importance must be discussed here.

Whether your first date is for a *cup of coffee, lunch, happy hour or dinner,* don't try and kiss a woman at the end of this get-together. A hug may be appropriate if there's some chemistry. Kisses will come later if all goes well.

I have learned many lessons while meeting many men. I never like being rude, but I have to admit that there were times when it became necessary. It's all about respect in my book!

Never Prolong the Inevitable

It's just not wise to prolong the agony of an ill-fated date or relationship. I have done this one time too many by trying to be respectful.

Let me tell you about Mr. Coupon Man. It is difficult to impress a woman when the coupon you present to the barista at Starbucks does not cover the cost of your date's cup of coffee.

Awkward and uncomfortable, I made it a very short-lived meet and greet. I believe the date lasted ten minutes.

I feel compelled to tell you that if Starbucks is above your monetary means, ask your date to meet you at McDonald's. She either will or she will not join you. Sorry gentlemen, I am far from being a snob, but I would end this date before it began. I am just not into McDonald's.

I certainly have no problem using coupons, but there is a time and a place. A first date is not the time or place unless it is someone you know as a friend or past acquaintance.

After you fall in love and become an item, go to Groupon and enjoy those trusty coupons, but I repeat, not on the first date.

Now to the other end of the spectrum. I went in one week from Mr. Coupon Man to Mr. Chauvinist.

I spoke with and met a very nice looking man on the Internet. We had iced tea at Starbucks and then went to dinner next door to a nice southwest restaurant called Z-Tejas.

Conversation started out interesting, but went downhill from there. He was a man of wealth and he wanted me to know it. He bragged about his palatial mansion in the hills of Paradise Valley. All of this was fine, but then it became strange.

He told me that his brother was a successful jeweler and that when he took his women out on dates, he not only told them what to wear, he adorned them with jewels "for the night."

I thanked him for dinner and ran the other way. What is with these men wanting to date and recreate women? I have always been told I dress well and I do it all by myself. Unreal.

For every reason I am discussing and more, I advise everyone to meet in public places. It's all about your safety. Please always make this a priority.

How are you going to get to know each other on a first date unless the both of you engage in conversation? It seems so simple, but is difficult for many.

I direct these comments to you, gentlemen. I still believe that women in their sixties appreciate chivalry. I know I do. Open the car door for your date; bring her a rose; pull out her chair at dinner and pay the restaurant bill.

This is a great beginning, in most cases. If, as a woman, you are still living in the Gloria Steinem era of equality (you pay half the bill; he pays half the bill), so be it. Keep in mind, however, that you ruin it for those of us who appreciate being treated like ladies.

You can elect to share your expenses after you marry, but not on that first date.

Gentlemen, don't just talk to the women you are dating. Listen to them. Remember, when a man is attentive and listens to a woman, he gives her a very special gift. You don't even need coupons for this gift. A little levity here.

Conversation evokes interest. This will be where an attraction can begin or end. When the positives or negatives of a person are discussed, begin by asking and answering questions.

Keep in mind that honesty and respect are key elements here. You do not have to divulge every story or secret from your past when first meeting. Certainly do not start off with a pack of lies.

In fact, you should refrain from elaborating on your life's experiences. Keep conversation light and fun. Talk about the positives in your lives: family, pet, travel, dining experiences and other likes and desires.

If you are legally separated, as was Good Time Charlie Brown when I met him, be honest and upfront with your date about your situation.

This was a bone of contention for me from the beginning to the end of my marriage. Your marital status is a key element. It is something that needs to be told to someone you may have interest in dating more than once. It's wrong not to reveal it to someone who thinks you are divorced.

Another issue of importance, for both men and women, is to leave your baggage in the past. It can and will interfere with a new person you are dating. You have to make the decision as to what baggage you need to leave behind and what baggage to continue carrying into your new life.

I met this handsome, charismatic man who carried way too much baggage for me. We had a great first date. I loved that his interests were vast. He was a retired pilot, worked on Wall Street and now owns his own film production company.

He was interesting; we were bonding until I learned he could not let go of his baggage from his marriage fifteen years ago. I did like him, but it was not worth my time and energy. I knew it would not work.

Always use your intuition. If something does not seem right, it probably is not. It's been said that: "Not everyone you lose is a loss."(Power of Positivity). Wow! Think about this.

It's also been said that: "If your absence doesn't affect them, then your presence never mattered" (Power of Positivity). This has been a hard one for me to handle. I know, however, that it is real.

It is something we have to deal with in life when relationships dissolve. Your intuition assists you in seeing negative as well as positive signs. Be conscious of it!

Live with positivity; live with happiness and joy; live in the now. We cannot change our yesterdays.

Yesterday contributes to who we are today, but it is essential to remember that today is a new day, a new start in life. Live it to the fullest!

If you are broken and a mate does not run away, but stays and helps put the pieces back together, you have a keeper.

I am looking for that wonderful man who knows all of my flaws and loves me in spite of them. Isn't this the type of love we all desire?

STEP 5

ALWAYS PROTECT YOUR IDENTITY

It's a different world. The Sexagenarians did not grow up with cell phones, computers and social media.

We grew up in a world without the technology of today. We were fortunate if we had a radio and a television, and our televisions were not flat screens with cable. How times have changed.

Today you meet someone; tell him or her your first and last name and before you know it, your full identity can be revealed from birth to present time. It's truly unbelievable.

I found this out early on when I began my dating experiences in Arizona.

I met a nice man at a Calculated Couples dance. Whenever we went to events sponsored by this group, we always danced together.

He invited me at one of the dances to go out to dinner at a country western restaurant in Scottsdale. I accepted.

I told him I would give him my address and phone number at the end of the dance. He told me "I already have it." I looked at him and asked where he got it. I knew I did not give it to him.

This was when I learned about search engines. These are Internet sites where anyone can go to research background information on anyone. I am certain this can be beneficial in many instances, but I found it invasive and did not appreciate that he did this without my consent.

Women, especially, never give your last name, address or any other personal information when first meeting someone. This includes your social security number, driver's license or other financial information.

I have always been a very trusting person. Not anymore. I have learned my lesson and I want you to be aware that if you, too, are a trusting person, you can be taken advantage of very easily. Reveal what you choose to reveal when the time is right and the person is the right person.

Are you a computer savvy Sexagenarian? I can type at the speed of lightening, but I am not an expert with today's technology. Thank goodness for my son and daughter who always lend me their expertise when I have computer problems.

As the majority of you already know, computers are our link to the outside world. As fulfilling and wonderful as they can be, they can also cause us problems.

I was recently hacked by a serious Trojan virus. Viruses can steal all of your personal information and use it in detrimental ways. Exercise caution at all times whether it is on the computer or live and in person.

If you have a computer, but are uncertain about using it for Internet dating, I certainly understand.

Mark Twain said, "A man cannot be comfortable without his own approval." Internet dating is not for everyone. It will definitely expand your horizon in meeting people, but if it does not feel right for you, then don't use it as a means of communication. The bottom line is to always protect your identity.

Age is but a Number

Why is so much emphasis put on a number? There are forty-year old people who are old in their ways. There are eighty-year old people who are young in their ways.

I choose to be a healthy, spirited Sexagenarian who enjoys life to its fullest today. My numeric age has no meaning. It does not identify me.

You are reading **Six Sexy, Simple Steps for Dating at Sixty;** therefore, I am making the assumption that you are a vibrant, exciting person who also chooses to live a happy, healthy life. Part of your happiness can and will be the dating world. Once you have read all of the steps, you will see how simple and fun the whole process will be.

Something important to interject here is the fact that you will not be attracted to every person you date and every person will not be attracted to you.

This revelation can be bothersome to both sexes. It's merely a reality of life. It's not because of your age, it's not because of your personality, it's not because of anything in particular, it just is.

So if you get turned down for a second date, move on and know that it was not meant to be.

Do not put on your "sensitive" hat and hide in a corner. The attraction was not there. It's just part of the game of love. It's the old *"Win Some; Lose Some."*

You are now getting closer to Mr. or Ms. Right. Enjoy meeting and greeting new people and prepare for your next date.

An issue that is troubling to many is age category dating. What do I mean by this? We have long accepted older men dating younger women. It's always been this way. It is not going to change. The reasoning behind it is different for all parties involved. It is not for me to question why this scenario takes place more often than not. It just does.

Today, however, we are seeing a reversal in behavior. Cougars, women in their forties and older, are dating younger men. Like it or not, this is acceptable behavior and it's here to stay.

I have encountered some interesting situations regarding men who will only date significantly older women. We all have choices in this area.

I made reference earlier to a gentleman I dated where there was no chemistry. He shared that his last relationship was with a woman thirty years younger than him. Hmmm, I always have my suspicions when a man who is in his sixties dates a woman in her thirties. I failed to mention that this man is a person of wealth.

He told me that he knew the relationship would not work from the beginning. I have to believe that it fulfilled whatever needs both she and he had at that time.

Another gentleman I dated was in his sixties. He, too, was very successful. He was a contractor in Las Vegas, Nevada. I liked him, but I am not into men who are smokers, let alone heavy smokers, so this was one problem for me.

He shared many of his success stories with me. He told me his preference is to date younger women. His last wife was half his age. He said she spent thousands of dollars on her clothing and did not worry about it because she was spending his money. How was I supposed to respond? I just put that smile on my face.

It's a choice we are all free to make. I did not ask him why he asked me out when it was obvious I was not in my twenties or thirties. I am, however, attractive; I am well maintained; and I am intelligent. Maybe that was part of the problem. I am intelligent.

One humorous part of our conversation was when he told me that he received tickets to a Smokey Robinson concert at one of the big hotels in Las Vegas. He asked his ex-wife if she would like to go with him. She said, "Who is Smokey Robinson?" Are you kidding me? I would have gone to this concert in a minute. No questions asked. Smokey Robinson is one of the greatest rhythm and blues soul artists to grace our concert stages and she knew nothing about this incredible talent.

Arm candy is arm candy is arm candy. Need I say more? We all have the right to make our own choices. I am still not certain why he invited me on a date. I was not thirty years his junior.

If I encounter a situation like this again, I will definitely ask more questions.

If it is your ego that defines who you are or proclaim to be, you need to think about your own self-doubt. The late, renown Dr. Dwayne W. Dyer speaks about this in his book "The Power of Intention Learning to Co-Create Your World Your Way." He says: "When you attempt to live by the low standards of your ego, you are a hostage to that very same ego. Your worth as a person is measured by your acquisitions and accomplishments." I will always have great respect for Dr. Dyer! His books are wonderful keepsakes.

Are you living up to the intention of having respect for yourself? Something to think about when you re-enter the dating scene. Of course, once again, the choice is yours.

STEP 6

FRIENDS, PARTNERS, LOVERS

Meeting new friends is wonderful. Meeting a friend, who can turn in to a life-long friend and eventually a life-long partner, is the best. There is an old saying; I do not know the source, but it goes like this: "Some people come into your life for a reason; some people come into your life for a season; some people come into your life for a life time."

A life time of friendship is unbeatable. The best way to start a new relationship is to first become friends. Get to know one another. Share interests. This process takes time, but so what? You are doing it with a friend who can become your partner for life.

The more you get to know about your friend, the closer you become. Of course, this can go the other way as well. If "friends" cannot agree on likes, interests and many other issues, it is best for this information to be discovered in the early stages of dating.

Is there a time parameter for being friends? It depends on the individual who is giving you the advice. I believe that it takes at least six months to get to know a person. This is merely my opinion.

Some folks have met their life-long partners and married within a few months after meeting. After twenty years, they are still happily married. It can happen, but it is not the norm.

Times have changed. We are a restless society today. If things do not go the way we like in a relationship or marriage, we put an end to it and move on to another. Sometimes we go solo. I speak from experience here.

Friendship is a great beginning. Just remember, it can easily lead to the next adventure, which can be the meeting of partners.

Partners can be with or without benefits. The term "Partners with Benefits" usually means it involves sexual relations. The couple must decide what is best at this point in time.

If your relationship is in the partnership phase, it is advancing to a positive place. Are you exclusive with one another or are there still other partners involved in both of your lives? This is a serious question.

Have you or have you not had sexual relations yet? Just how much do you really know about your partner? How many previous partners have each of you been with sexually? Have you practiced safe sex? This is some serious stuff. It should not be taken lightly.

Steve Harvey, the wonderful comedienne and CLO (Chief Love Officer), tells women: "Do not give up the cookie for at least ninety days." Steve refers to women as *treasures*. He's right. We are treasures!

No one can tell anyone when the time is right "to give up the cookie," but the essence of this statement is that individuals should get to know one another before having sexual relations.

An older woman who was sitting in Steve's audience asked him if this rule also pertained to the senior population. Steve said, "Hell No!" "You don't have time to waste."

Laugh if you will. I can only say that when it's right, it's right. I am not out for a romp in the hay at this juncture of my life. I know what is important to me, so I choose to proceed with caution rather than regret.

I am looking for genuine love. I desire a selfless man who knows how to truly show love and affection to his partner, and it must be unconditional. My marriage to Good Time

Charlie Brown was always conditional. As long as I followed his lead, all was well.

This was *not* a partnership. It's just one more reason why my marriage failed.

Decide when you are dating if you are looking for long-term love or short-term lust. I vote for long term love.

Affirmations, Vision Board

I am going to discuss an area that may be unfamiliar to you. I briefly mentioned this earlier. It's called affirmations. You simply get a piece of paper or tablet and write down all your desires. If it pertains to your future mate, write in the *now*.

For example, some of my many affirmations are: "I am happy, healthy and prosperous; Everything I need comes in the perfect time; Where I am there is all good; I fall in love!"

I write these affirmations down ten times each day. Sometimes I choose to verbalize them rather than write them. This is a powerful process and it works.

You must do it for a minimum of thirty days. If these affirmations do not turn into reality after thirty days, don't fret. Sometimes it will take a great deal longer, but do not stop.

If some of your affirmations do not occur, then they were not meant to come to fruition. It just means that something better is in store for you. You have to *"Believe"* and apply this process for it to work. Honest; it's powerful!

In addition to writing or reciting your affirmations daily, you may want to consider creating a vision board. It's another excellent tool to assist you in your search for that truly awesome person in your life.

To some, this may sound like a ridiculous thing to do. For any of you who have done it, you know that it works. I always have an updated vision board that is on the wall in my bedroom. I review it every morning and every evening to ensure I am on task.

If you do not know what a vision board is, let me explain. It's a large piece of poster board. Select whatever color suits you. You can purchase the poster board at a Dollar Store or craft store. Gather all the magazines you have in your home. If you do not have any, go to your local grocery or big box store and purchase about one-half dozen magazines with lots of wonderful pictures.

The pictures you are looking for depict what you want to see happen in your life. For example, I selected a picture of a convertible Sports car (just so happens I really do own a convertible Sports car). A happy couple is in this car smiling, with the top down, while enjoying their ride together. I desire this type of happiness. Don't we all?

I also cut out positive sayings such as: "Power Your Purpose," "Happiness," "Love," "Be Good to Yourself Each and Every Day." I put these sayings all over my board.

Cut out any pictures you desire that will enhance your happiness. In addition to love, it can be a wad of money you desire. If this is something important to you, cut it out and put it on your vision board.

The vision board can denote good health, love and monetary gain. You are the creator; you decide what you want to see in your life today and tomorrow.

Fill this poster with pictures and sayings that make you feel joyful. Your dreams and wishes will come true. Maybe not today. Be patient; you will see results. As I previously mentioned, if some of these vision board wishes or affirmations do not occur, then I repeat, these were not meant to come to fruition. Others will and they will be more beneficial.

Add new wishes and affirmations as you desire. Be patient and remain positive. I cannot use the word positive enough times! It's the difference between success and failure.

I am a believer because it has worked over and over again for me. What do you have to lose? Just keep in mind, the seeds you plant and nurture today will flourish and grow tomorrow. "Life is a magnet for all that is positive; it moves forward with positive attitude and actions." This is quoted from Seeds of Positivity.

I can tell you I live a happy, fulfilled life today. I would not be truthful if I didn't say that I feel it would be even more complete if I had a wonderful man in my life.

I follow the *Six Sexy, Simple Steps for Dating at Sixty* because these steps work! I am seeking just as you are, to find my honest, genuine true love. I know he is out there waiting for me to walk through the door.

We all deserve the best in our lives. Never settle for anything less. Love is team work; love is giving and receiving; love is unconditional not superficial; love is honest; love is one of the strongest, most wonderful feelings two people can share with one another.

Be Selective, Be Real

If you have any doubts or questions at all about your partner's sexual past, it would behoove you to request that he or she be tested for sexually transmitted diseases. This is an insurance policy for both of you. It's *just a sign of the times.*

Be patient. Be selective. Be real. If your desire is to have true love, you will have it. I believe the best is yet to come and I am travelling on this road with you.

Be happy. Enjoy your life. Live it to the fullest. Make your dreams come true. Get out there and start dating, Sexagenarians. You have the six steps; use them and have a great time.

Send your questions or remarks to my website: www.stepstodating.at60.love. I look forward to blogging with you.

My best to all Sexagenarians who embark on this fun and sexy dating journey!

Chele Iam

SAY "YES" TO ALL THE POSITIVES. SAY "NO" TO ALL THE NEGATIVES. THIS IS YOUR WONDROUS JOURNEY. MAKE IT JOYFUL; MAKE IT MEANINGFUL!

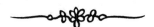

YOUR SIXTIES CAN BE THE BEST
TIME OF YOUR LIFE!

*EVERY PERSON COMES INTO YOUR
LIFE FOR A REASON!*

WE ATTRACT WHAT WE DESIRE!

WHAT WE THINK WE FEEL;
WHAT WE FEEL WE BELIEVE!

LOVE YOURSELF. TRUST YOUR INSTINCTS. KNOW THAT YOU DESERVE THE BEST!

CHOOSE YOUR DESTINY.
FOLLOW YOUR DREAMS!

DATING NOTES

 *DATING NOTES*

 *DATING NOTES*

DATING NOTES

DATING NOTES

DATING NOTES

DATING NOTES

DATING NOTES

Printed in the United States
by Bookmasters

Printed in the United States
By Bookmasters